Josiah Nicholas Kidd

Silvanus and Ruth

The Operations of Providence with Respect to Matrimony

Josiah Nicholas Kidd

Silvanus and Ruth
The Operations of Providence with Respect to Matrimony

ISBN/EAN: 9783337405533

Printed in Europe, USA, Canada, Australia, Japan

Cover: Foto ©Lupo / pixelio.de

More available books at **www.hansebooks.com**

SILVANUS AND RUTH,

OR THE

OPERATIONS OF PROVIDENCE

WITH RESPECT TO

MATRIMONY.

BY

REV. JOSIAH NICHOLAS KIDD.

PARSONS, KANSAS:
THE FOLEY PRINTING COMPANY.
1897

PREFACE.

The most of this little poem was composed about ten years ago. By several friends, it was then pronounced worthy of publication. The author, however, not being sufficiently satisfied, and not having time to finish and revise it, laid it aside for some future time. The passing years being so heavily laden with other work, the poem was compelled to remain in solitude until about two weeks ago, when Providence opened up the way and the Muses came again to assist in revising and finishing it. It is now sent forth to the public with the prayer that it will glorify God, and be entertaining and helpful to both young and old.

J. N. KIDD.

Parsons, Kansas, June 15, 1897.

Go, my first born little book,
Go to ev'ry place and nook,
Go to ev'ry girl and boy,
Go with comfort, peace and joy,
Go with entertainment true,
Go with good instruction, too:
Go to youth and hoary age,
Go to poet and to sage,
Go to all beneath the sun,
Go with blessings for each one.

In old Ohio's grand domain,
  Where valleys, rich with fruit and grain,
Lie down between the sloping hills
To drink from rivers, creeks and rills,
That crops may on their bosom grow,
A child was born not high nor low,
But like the creek between its banks,
He took his place in human ranks.
'Twas not in April nor in May,
When nature looked sublime and gay,
And greeted man with smiling face,
And welcomed him with fond embrace,
But when cold winter, bleak and bare,
With snowy feet and long white hair,
Stepped in ahead the vernal spring,
And deadened every living thing.
While nature shivered with the cold,
And parents both were growing old,
The guardian angel came with joy,
And took control their little boy.
He guarded him through infant days,
From all the danger of his ways,

And followed him through coming years,
And wiped away his childish tears.
Then by and by with swiftest gait,
He searched for him a future mate.
He left him in the safest care,
Of other angels bright and fair,
And spread his wings and flew away
Upon an early day in May,
To look among the daughters fair,
Of rosy cheeks and auburn hair.
For one who would a help-meet be,
And bring the boy felicity.
Throughout the state of Ohio,
And then, New England, he doth go :
And while he's sailing swift and fast,
He meets another unsurpassed
In flowing robes of spotless white,
And face resplendent with delight.
They both in salutation bend,
And seem to fully comprehend
The other's thoughts and hopes and aim,
And that their mission is the same.

Then with one voice they both exclaim—
Their hearts with heaven's love aflame—
Let us go down to yonder mount,
And on its summit there recount
Our work, our mission and our aims,
And also learn each other's names.
Then round and round and lower down,
They sailed in long white flowing gown,
Until they reached the little hill,
(Which nestled by a gushing rill)
All covered oe'r with forest trees
That rustled in the gentle breeze.
So down they sat upon the ground,
On top that lovely shady mound,
And like two lovers side by side,
Talked of a future groom and bride.
With loving hearts and sparkling eyes,
They sweetly talk of marriage ties,
And tell their names and station too;
Also the work they came to do.

Fidelia, was the name of one,
Who shone with brilliance like the sun,

And Rupert, was the other's name,
Who was of great angelic fame.

While human sex does not belong,
To heaven's bright angelic throng,
Yet may we not to them ascribe,
(To suit the purpose of the scribe,
And limitations of our state,
While subject to this blessed fate)
Some male and female qualities,
Less human technicalities ?
Still other reasons might be named
To keep the scribe from being blamed,
But they will all appear in time,
Expressed in story and in rhyme.
But now the story must unfold,
And all its wondrous facts be told.

The angel of the sterner kind
Described the girl he hoped to find ;
And as he talked of this and that,
The fem'nine angel raptly sat,
And like a modest maiden dame,

Exclaimed, " I know her, and her name.
I saw her born of humble birth,
The sweetest girl on all the earth,
With eyes both dyed in heaven's blue,
And hair of purest auburn hue.
Though yet a babe in mother's arms,
I see in her the future charms,
Which, like the fabled Siren muse,
Will never let her husband loose.
But hold him fast in loves embrace
And pour sweet smiles into his face,
Until relentless death shall break
The ties which purest love did make.
From heaven, I was sent to earth,
As guardian angel from her birth,
To guide her through this world of sin,
And teach her how the crown to win
Of female virtue pure and white
Until she basks in heaven's light.
I left her in another's care
So I would feel no doubt or fear,
And started out among the sons,

To watch the course of life that runs
In sweeping currents through their veins,
Producing muscles, bones and brains,
From which the actions of their life
Spring forth in either peace or strife,
To see if I could find a youth,
Prepared by God for little Ruth."

"Praise God, Fidelia," Rupert said,
With crown of gold raised from his head:
" The little boy I have in care,
Of ruddy visage, bright and fair,
And brawn and muscle firm and strong,
And mind intent to shun the wrong,
I think will be a proper youth,
To mate your darling little Ruth.
If you will come and go with me
To where the oak and poplar tree,
The sugar maple and the beech,
With loud and shrilling voices schreech,
And gently wave their vernal fans,
And beckon to the other clans

Which round them like an army strong,
With hands so small and arms so long,
To join with them in glad refrain
Because the Spring has come again,
I'll show you where Silvanus dwells,
Among the forest trees and dells."

"I will," Fidelia quickly said,
Instinct with sure success ahead.

"Then let us," Rupert said, "arise
Up toward the blue and tranquil skies,
And through the lovely azure plain,
Sail oe'r yon lofty mountain chain,
And toward Ohio haste away,
For it is now the close of day."

Then from the lovely shady mount,
Where on they sat in old Vermont,
They raised their wings and took their flight
In flowing robes of spotless white,
Which floated back beneath their feet,
Upon the gentle breeze most sweet.

With long extended glossy wings
All covered oe'r with shining rings ;
And crowns of beauty on their heads
Adorned with pearls on golden threads,
And faces brilliant as the sun,
When he his course doth proudly run,
They glided on with lightning speed,
Oe'r mountains tall and flow'ry mead,
Until they reached the humble dome,
Where young Silvanus made his home.
The sun had run his daily race,
And hid his bright refulgent face,
That other worlds might come in sight,
To beautify the sombre night ;
And Ebon from his starry throne,
With many blessings all his own,
Had rocked the busy world to sleep,
And from the heat of day did keep
It resting in the gentle breeze,
That played among the forest trees,
When these two angels ope'd the door
And gently walked across the floor

Until they reached the trundle bed,
On which the boy in slumber laid.
There bright Fidelia stood and gazed,
With heart in prayer to heaven raised,
For wisdom and for help divine,
To ascertain the Lord's design.
Her prayer was heard, the answer came,
And lit the future with its flame.
With microscopic sight she read
Just how the little boy was bred,
And saw his life in conduct flow
Through all his journey here below.
With pensive eyes she looked beyond,
And saw his future as it dawned
Into deportment, act and thought,
And how he would be trained and taught.
Her heart with joy began to swell,
And sparkling eyes began to tell,
That she had found the precious prize,
Of proper age and proper size,
In that delightfnl ruddy youth,
Prepared by God for little Ruth;

And turning round took Rupert's arm,
And glided out without alarm,
To have a pleasant talk with him,
Upon a long and swinging limb,
Which from a beach tree reached afar,
As if to see a shining star.
Upon that limb they sweetly sat,
And talked of this and then of that,
Concerning ycung Silvanus' life,
And she, who was to be his wife.

With modest voice, Fidelia said,
"Your boy I've seen and fully read,
And found in him the virtues true,
Which will, the life of Ruth imbue,
With satisfaction joy and love,
Allied to that in realms above.
And now if you will go with me,
We'll leave this sweet delightful tree,
And this sublime ambrosial land,
Where Cupid waves his magic wand,
To captivate Calliope,

The muse who reigns oe'r poetry;
And to the west we'll quickly go,
Where rivers through the prairies flow,
And fertile plains like oceans broad,
To beautify the works of God,
Spread out in grandeur like the skies,
When on their bosom no cloud flies ;
And there upon the prairie strand,
Near where it joins a small woodland,
I'll show you Ruth's abiding place,
And let you read her lovely face."

"With pleasure I will go with you,"
Said Rupert, " for I must be true
To him whose happiness I seek,
And he of whom I love to speak."

Then from the limb they rose aloft,
Upon the gentle breeze so soft,
That even night-birds could not hear
Their silent motions through the air;
And toward the west in rapid flight,
They sailed on that delightful night

To Illinois, the destined place,
Toward which they now had set their face.
The sky was clear, the air was calm,
And filled with nature's sweetest balm.
The queen of night was on her throne,
And in sublimest beauty shone,
With full round face of amber glow,
Upon the landscapes far below.
Ten thousand worlds appeared in space,
With each a bright and shining face,
To beautify the vernal night.
On which the angles took their flight.
The scenes below and scenes above,
They pass between on wings of love,
And sing with joy this glad refrain
While gliding through the azure plain :

" How bright the love of God doth shine,
Upon the earth below !
For all the stars of heav'n combine,
His loving face to show.

Oh see the worlds in splendor roll,
Like flaming balls of fire,

As God unfolds his shining scroll,
To let the earth admire !

Let shining worlds his praises sing ;
Let angels join the choir ;
Let all the earth its homage bring,
In love's sublime attire.

Sing on, sing on, Oh universe,
In endless praise, sing on,
And let your song God's love rehearse,
Through Jesus Christ His Son.''

So on they go with flaming zeal,
Their eyes aglow with heaven's weal,
And songs of praise that far excel,
What Orpheus could write or tell,
And conversation free and pure,
Concerning their great overture,
Until they reach the cottage home,
Where guardian angels love to roam,
To catch a glimpse of little Ruth,
To see if she might be, forsooth,
The girl they longed and hoped to find
To mate the boy they left behind.

The weary world was still asleep,
Excepting those compelled to weep,
Because of death's relentless stroke,
Which had their social circle broke.

The humble cottage snugly stood,
Near where the prairie joined the wood,
Upon a gentle sloping mound,
With ornamental trees around.
So in they went without a noise—
Their hearts athrob with untold joys—
And soon they stood beside the bed,
On which the lovely Ruth was laid,
Between her parents safe from harm,
And sleeping on her mother's arm.

There Rupert stood with gleaming eyes,
Fixed on the girl, and then the skies,
For well he knew, that from above,
True wisdom, like the Holy Dove,
Must come and throw prophetic light,
Upon his vision and his sight.
The keen prophetic vision came,

And lit the future with its flame,
The same as when Fidelia prayed,
And young Silvanus life portrayed,
He saw her life through every stage,
From childhood down to ripe old age,
And read her thoughts and motives too,
From which he very quickly knew,
That he had found the girl he sought,
With all the female virtues fraught,
Who would a faithful helpmeet be,
And bring his boy felicity,
With smiling face he turned about,
And with Fidelia glided out
To have another talk with her,
About the things that should occur
To cause the boy and girl to meet,
When preparations were complete.

So down upon the lawn they sat
Beneath the starry skies to chat;
And there upon the lovely grass
They talked of what should come to pass—

How boy and girl should both be led—
Until the time that they should wed.

The time and all were fixed upon,
When Rupert said; "I must be gone;
But let us first, before we part,
In prayer and praise lift up our heart
To Him whose will we love to do,
And He whose face we love to view,
And who has blessed us with success,
And filled our cup with happiness."
Then down upon the grass they knelt,
The sight of which a heart would melt,
And offered up a thankful prayer,
Which bounded upward through the air.

They gently rose from off their knees,
And talked awhile beneath the trees,
Like friends before they separate,
When one's about to emigrate.

At length their conversation closed,
And Rupert first farewells proposed:

Rupert:
"Farewell, Fidelia, I must go
Fack to my charge in Ohio.
May heavens joys thy bosom swell,
As I again, say, fare thee well ;
And may you crown the life of Ruth,
With peace and joy and love and truth."

Fidelia :
" Dear Rupert, I shall ne'er forget
The time when yesterday we met,
And talked about our little pets,
And crowned them with such epithets,
That we, without a doubt believed
Our undertaking was accheived.
And then, our supramundane flight,
On this delightful vernal night,
Has been so full of peace and joy,
Because we've found our girl and boy,
That I must say my heart doth sing,
More gladly than the birds of Spring.
And now we part to meet again

Upon this lovely western plain,
When you and young Silvanus come,
And locate near Ruth's happy home.
So fare-thee-well, with greatest cheer,
Come see me once or twice a year;
Then I will come and visit you,
And thus we can our work review.''

Rupert :
'' Well said, Fidelia, fare-thee-well,
The joy I feel no tongue can tell;
But now I can no longer stay,
For long before the break of day,
I must Silvanus' dwelling reach
Among the maples and the beech.

Then Rupert spread his glossy wings,
All covered o'er with shining rings,
And like a brilliant lightening-flash,
Without its rolling thunder clash,
Or like a meteoric stone
From some exploded planet thrown,
He went a sailing through the air,

With such a glory, such a glare,
That bright Fidelia stood and gazed.
Until the ground between was raised
Above the line he sailed upon,
And he below the sky was gone.

The moon was still upon her throne,
When faithful Rupert. all unknown
To those within the house asleep,
Across the floor did gently sweep,
And took control his boy again,
To lead him through this world of sin.

Both fam'lies rose at break of day,
Unconscious of the grand display
Of holy angels in the room,
With happy faces all abloom
With heavens bright immortal youth,
And love, and wisdom. joy and truth.
The morning birds began to sing,
And make the woods with music ring.
The sun arose with smiling face,
Expressive of benignant grace,

And shed his glory on the earth,
And to another day gave birth.
The busy world, renewed by rest,

Again its muscles puts to test.
The wheels of commerce roll along
With rattling, clanging, ringing song.
And thus the world from day to day,
Rolled onward in its destined way,
Imparting poverty and wealth,
Affliction, sorrow, joy and health,
According to a higher plan
Which man can only partly scan.

Amid these scenes of grief and joy,
The angels raised their girl and boy,
And led them in the ordained way,
To meet on their appointed day.

In early youth they sought the Lord,
Believed in Christ and in his Word,
Obtained the pardon of their sin,
And started out the crown to win

Of everlasting life and peace,
Where pleasures evermore increase.

To district school they both were sent,
And there their time was partly spent
While passing through the early stage
Of happy youths florescent age.

The earth rolled on around the sun,
To where it first its race begun,
And then again it took its flight,
Around the central orb of light,
And so continued once a year,
Completing its ordained career,
Producing seasons richly fraught
With blessings which it wisely sought
In regions of celestial heights,
For man, the object of its flights.

A few such revolutions passed,
The boy and girl arrive at last,
To that important stage of life,
When thoughts of husband and of wife,
Become the silent motor force

Propelling them along the course
That leads to that connubial state,
Which they, with joy, anticipate.
Unconscious of the others name,
And knowing not the others aim,
Nor what the country or the place,
Or what the visage of the face,
They both, at length, arise and start,
Though many hundred miles apart,
Upon the hymenean route,
With secret purpose fixed and mute,
To seek the partner of their life —
The husband true and faithful wife.
They thought sometimes that they had
    found,
The one to whom they could be bound,
But something always interfered,
And all their present prospects seared.
They calmly bore the consequence,
Believing that God's providence
Was guiding them in all their way,
And that he would, some future day,

Reveal the one they hoped to find,
Alike in ways, alike in mind.
Reflection soon revealed the fact,
That they the age and wisdom lacked
To fit them for the marriage state,
Which they in haste did meditate;
For tis a fact by age well known,
That love, when first upon the throne,
Is like a vacillating queen,
Who changes with the changing scene.

The days in quick succession fly,
The weeks and months grow old and die,
And ere another year rolls round,
A happy fam'ly westward bound,
Is seen on upland and on plain,
With young Silvanus in the train.
The covered wagon rolls along,
Conveying that domestic throng,
To Illinois, the western state,
To which they aimed to emigrate.
At length they reached the destined place,
Toward which they all had set their face,

And settled near the town of Booth,
Not more than twenty miles from Ruth.

'The angels now and then had met,
Without a failure to regret,
For holy angels never err
Like human beings everywhere :
And now, they are again to meet
When plans are all about complete.
Fidelia comes to be the guest,
And welcome Rupert to the west.

'Twas on a dark and stormy night
When all the stars from human sight
Were hid behind a thunder cloud,
Whose cannonading was so loud,
That some awoke in great dismay,
And some began to fear and pray.
Its darting flames, the heavens rent,
As if it devastation meant.
But yet the angels did not fear
The mighty storm or lightning spear—
Nor all the shafts from heaven thrown—

For danger was to them unknown.
Silvanus' parents siezed with fright,
Arose in haste the lamp to light ;
But Rupert whispered in their ear :
"Lie down in peace and do not fear,
Or wake the children from their sleep,
For God is near their souls to keep.
He guides the lightning in its course;
Controls the wind's vehement force:
So trust in His almighty arm,
And he will save you from all harm."
Then back to bed they went again,
And heard no more the wind and rain.

Ere long Fidelia came and knocked,
And Rupert quick the door unlocked.
They both with joy each other greet,
In tones with melody replete,
And then they talk of providence
In lofty strains of eloquence,
Which poets, though they all combine,
And call upon the Muses nine,

Can only poorly imitate,
And only partially relate.

Fidelia in her loving style,
Her face illumined with a smile,   .
Describes her journey through the storm,
And how its forces did perform.

Fidelia:
"With yonder cloud I came to-night,
To see the bright electric light
By atmospheric force displayed,
And by dynamic force conveyed
In zigzag streams of living fire,
Disporting with Uterpe's choir
Across the heavens with a noise,
Expressive of transporting joys.
Above, below and all around,
I heard the praise of God resound,
And saw his glory flashing forth,
From east to west, from south to north;
And while I came on through the storm,
Beholding natures laws perform

The will of him who reigns supreme,
And who devised the wondrous scheme,
My admiration grew so great,
That I began to celebrate,
With demonstrations of delight,
His goodness, glory and his might,
And chant the music of the spheres,
Which fell so sweetly on my ears."

Rupert:
"I'm glad. Fidelia, you have come,
To see me in my western home.
I saw you coming in the cloud,
And heard your voice resounding loud
Amidst that labyrinthal scene,
The like of which I've often seen ;
And every time I see the sight,
It fills my heart with new delight.
But now, Fidelia, while I love
To talk about those scenes above,
And how Omnipotence controls
The storm which frightens human souls,
But fills the angels with delight

31

As they behold the wondrous sight,
I must, our conversation turn,
To something which doth more concern
Our mission to this mundane sphere,
To guide a girl and boy's career
Until their earthly race is run,
And they ascend above the sun."

Fidelia :
"For this, dear Rupert, I have come,
And this, my long exordium
Was to the subject introduce,
And from it, then, the fact deduce,
That Providence, in love, controls,
Not only storms but human souls,
When they are seeking for a mate,
Though some men call it luck and fate.
But yet the fact remains the same,
And God will glorify his name
In each divine unfolding plan,
Concerning weak and sinful man.
The first man, Adam, found a mate,
But not by chance or luck or fate ;

For God prepared her for the man,
According to his ordained plan.
This same eternal purpose runs
To all his multitudes of sons—
That God with wisdom and with care,
Doth for each soul a mate prepare—
That in the sacred marriage rite,
Most men and women shall unite.
And if they seek with cautious care,
They'll find that God is always near
To give direction to their feet
That they, the proper one may meet."

Rupert ;
"'Tis true. Fidelia," Rupert said,
" That men and women are to wed.
And if they wed with proper care,
They'll have no cause to shed a tear,
Or to regret their marriage vow ;
For love will be the fruitful bough
That yields a pure domestic bliss,
And pardons every word amiss.
Their lives will soon melt into one

Beneath the warm refulgent sun—
That brightest orb in realms above—
Domestic, and true christian love.
Their peace will like a river flow,
Through all their journey here below,
Enlarging as it flows along,
Through realms of sorrow or of song.
We have a match like this to make,
Which naught but death can ever break—
A match which God himself hath planned,
As they will some day understand.
A few more years and they shall meet,
And form a union pure and sweet.

Fidelia ·   .
" Yes, Rupert, what you say is true,
Such cautious people never rue
The vow they made to love and share,
The others joy and grief and care.
Those matches made alone by self,
For worldly gain or paltry pelf,
And those made too with undue haste,
Without regard to proper taste,

And those who've been deceived also
By lovers false and outward show,
Are always sure to end their course,
In woeful strife or in divorce.
If they would only stop and think,
Before they-reach the fatal brink,
What consequences it involves,
Which neither life nor time absolves,
They, then, would heed the voice within
Which tells them how to seek and win
A partner of intrinsic worth,
Made such by nature and by birth ;
Or if they'd heed their angel guard,
Who labors with them, long and hard,
Or even take the good advice
Of those their seniors more than thrice,
Who've lived to see the bitter strife
Of injudicious married life,
They'd have occasion to rejoice,
And never would regret their choice."

Rupert :
" 'Tis true, Fidelia, and we know

That wealth, with all its pomp and show,
Can not evolve a true manhood—
Though wealth when not abused, is good,
And necessary in its place
To help advance the human race—
But yet 'tis virtue makes the man,
Because it doth his motives scan,
And makes them clean and pure and true,
So nothing evil may ensue.

Fidelia :
'' Yet Rupert, there is something more,
Which human nature must adore
Before it can attain the height
Of perfect manhood pure and white.
By nature man is all defiled,
Because he was by sin beguiled.
There's nothing that can extricate
The creature from his fallen state,
And purify his moral tone,
But Christianity alone. ''

Rupert :
'' Of course Fidelia, this is true,

And man cannot the fact undo.
The moral standard of the world,
Which learned sages have unfurled—
Though much of it I can commend,
Because it doth not God offend—
While it sets forth a moral plan
To make an upright honest man,
Can never pôw'r divine impart,
To purify the human heart.
It is a fact, divine and sure,
That man, in order to be pure,
Must have his heart renewed by grace,
And with true faith and love embrace
The All Sufficient Son of God,
Who did the sinner's winepress trod."

Fidelia :
" Religion is the source divine
Of all those blessings which combine
To make man happy, wise and good
In youth or age or strong manhood;
And if the nymphs, who contemplate
A leap into the marriage state,

Would only look for christain fruit
In those who ply the courtship suit,
They would not make the great mistake,
Which causes many hearts to ache ;
Or, vice versa, if the swains,
Would always take the proper pains,
They would not let the vain coquettes
Deceive them with their epithets,
For they would look for christain maids
Whose moral lustre never fades.
The swain and nymph we have in care,
Do each these christain virtues share,
And therefore, both of them shall find,
A union true of heart and mind."

This topic done, Fidelia said:
" Five happy hours have quickly fled
In sweet communion here with you;
And now I must bid you adieu
And to my happy post repair,
For morning's dawn will soon be here.

Rupert :
"But dear Fidelia, let me first,

Repeat the truth you first rehearsed ;
That Providence supremely reigns
O'er all these low terrestrial plains,
With such extensive amplitude,
And such sublime solicitude,
That man cannot its height ascend,
Or to its depth profound descend ;
And neither can the angels see
Its deep and vast immensity :
But we can see much more than man.
How God unfolds his righteous plan
In everything that appertains   ·
To human joys or human pains;
And since the sacred marriage rite,
Contributes to the worlds delight,
God's providence to it extends,
And to it all its blessings lends.
The angels do not wed, you know,
Like human beings here below;
But yet our unions suit our state,
And satisfy us with our fate.
To man alone, its blessings come,

And angels can not all them sum ;
But still we know they must be sweet,
"With peace and hope and joys replete.

Fidelia :
Dear Rupert this transporting theme,
Doth with increasing int'rest teem,
But I must now bid you adieu,
And close this pleasant interview."

Rupert :
" Farewell Fidelia, may our youth
Continue in the way of truth.
Oft now with pleasure we shall meet,
And often now each other greet."

The storm was o'er, the clouds were gone,
The twinkling stars in beauty shone,
The waning moon had just appeared,
With more than half her visage bleared,
And twilight, morning's herald gay,
Proclaimed the fast approaching day
When Ruperts fair celestial guest,

In heavens bright apparel dressed,
Arose into the ether plain,
And sped her way toward home again:
And as she swiftly sailed along
She sang an angel's mission song :

"Oh how blest the angels mission
To this fallen world below,
Which is bowed in deep submission
To Apollyons reign of woe ;
Sin has marred its ancient beauty,
Crushed the heart of man with grief,
Caused him to neglect his duty,
And has given no relief.

We are here with saints defending
God's eternal right to reign,
And with mighty fiends contending,
For his kingdom's lost domain ;
Soon Immanuel will be reigning
In the new created earth,
Not a fiend or foe remaing,
And no pain or woe or death.

Then the joyful acclamation,
Shall be heard by one and all :—
This is now full restoration,
And redemption from the fall ;
Alleluiah, blest condition!
Glory, honor to our king!
Alleluiah, blest fruition!
All ye saints and angels sing.''

This thought had so her mind engrossed,
That when she reached her happy post,
She still was singing loud and strong ·
But human ears heard not the song.

Their plans begin to soon unfold,
In ways both strange and manifold.
The youth's, impelled by strong desire,
A higher knowledge to acquire,
Go forth with expectations rife
To drink the cup of college life.
But ere their minds were satisfied,
They felt compelled to lay aside,
(Though not without solicitude)

The course of study they pursued.
But though their school day plans were
    gone,
Yet strong impulsions bore them on,
As anxious seekers in pursuit
Of wisdom's choice and blessed fruit.
As students they continued still
To drink their knowledge from the quill
Of ancient and of modern lore,
Until they had in mind a store
Of ready knowledge for their use,
In public life or in recluse.
And thus the current of their life,
Rolled on with aspirations rife,
Enlarging as it flowed along
Through sombre shades or realms of song
As every day poured in its cup,
And every year its wealth gave up.

The youths have now both reached an age,
When sober thoughts their minds engage,
Concerning that connubial state
Which erstwhile they did contemplate.

At length they both begin to muse,
Upon some strange but welcome news
Which comes to them through faithful
    friends
And Cupid's arrow through them sends.

Silvanus :
"Is what I hear an idle tale,
That comes on some unfriendly gale
To agitate my heart and mind
Until I can no respite find?
Or has some angel interposed,
And all these thoughts to me proposed ?
I learn by what some people say,
That there resides not far away,
A damsel of superior worth,
Though of an humble country birth ;
And whom true friends do recommend
As one to whom I should extend,
The friendly offer of my hand,
Though why? I cannot understand.
Somehow their story strikes me so,
That I do feel inclined to go,

44

And see if they have told the truth
About this damsel they call Ruth.
Eut yet I will not be in haste
The cup of deeper love to taste,
For now I feel the burning coal,
Through all the regions of my soul,
And if I see her now, I feel
That love would all my senses steal.
So then I'll wait till I regain
The full possession of my brain,
And till an opportunity
Makes way for such a liberty."

While he was thus in mind confused,
Ruth also in her parlor mused :

" 'Tis passing strange that what I hear
Falls with such force upon my ear,
And trills along on every nerve,
Until it captures the reserve
Which I have kept for only one,
Who lives somewhere beneath the sun.
I think Silvanus is the swain

For whom I've looked so long in vain ;
For never was my heart so swayed,
Since I was in the cradle laid.
Though I have never seen his face,
Affection's arms doth him embrace.
I wonder if its mysticism,
Or weird and dreamy Occultism,
That makes my heart to thus expand ?
Or is it some good angel hand,
Impregnate with electric fire,
Awaking in me this desire
Toward one, a stranger yet to me,
And whom, perhaps, I'll never see ?
Begone, ye weird and mystic band !
I'm sure it is an angel's hand,
For now I feel the holy touch,
And know full well there is none such,
Among your visionary crowd
So motley and so bold and loud."

Thus those two hearts in union beat
And longed to each the other meet ;
But something in between them stepped,

And in suspense they both were kept,
Until the time the angel's set,
When first the holy guardians met.

The fall and winter passed away,
And then the angels ope'd the way
For those two loving souls to meet,
And to each other kindly greet.
'Twas at a public meeting place
When first they saw each other's face.
The anxious throng from far and near
Had come religious truths to hear.
A faithful friend to both was there
And took occasion, with great care,
To introduce the waiting youth
And make them feel that of a truth
The other was a person who
Was honest, upright. faithful, true.
The angels, too, were there on hand,
To see that what they wisely planned,
Was executed with the skill,
Which would their hearts with true love
    thrill.

The work was done : the two youths met,
The way and time that long was set.
With conduct graceful and polite,
And faces flushing with delight,
They kindly talked as friend to friend,
And seemed to fully comprehend
The meaning of the other's look,
In which their hearts much pleasure took.
This pleasant meeting though but brief,
Was to their minds a great relief ;
For what they heard was now evinced,
And they were fully now convinced,
That they had found the one to whom
They could be bound as bride and groom.
But while their minds in this reposed,
Their separation soon disclosed
New feelings of solicitude,
Which called for stalwart fortitude.

Silvanus :
"I must confess," Silvanus mused,
"That I am very much confused,
And hardly know just what to do,

Or just what course I should pursue,
Or how to vent plethoric though*,
Concerning one who is so fraught
With such attractive gracefulness,
And such a charming loveliness.
The strength I summoned for a shield,
Doth now in sweet submission yield
To Love, the rightful queen of earth,
Whose peaceful, joyful, sacred birth
In Eden's pure and happy state,
Caused all the stars to celebrate.
As far as Love's dominion goes,
Peace, like a gentle river, flows,
And joys transporting fill the soul,
Because of her benign control ;
For when this queen is on her throne,
All strife and envy are unknown.
Within my heart she sits as queen,
With dignified and graceful mien,
And I do feel the blissful thrill,
Of her benignant sov'reign will.
She bids me, Ruth, at once to woo,

And at the court of Hymen sue
For full possession of her heart
And this important courtship start.
But how shall I begin this case ?
By letter, friend, or face to face ?
By letter, says a voice within,
Is just the way you should begin.
A letter, then, I'll quickly send,
And my respects to her extend.''

Ruth :

''Somehow,'' mused Ruth, ''I can't refrain
From thinking of that lovely swain,
With whom I met some time ago,
And whom I hope to better know.
If I were only loved by him,
My eyes in tears of joy would swim,
My heart would thrill with pure delight,
And I could rest in peace at night.
I never loved as I do now,
And never shall again I vow.
Silvanus is my only choice,
And with his love I could rejoice

In any circumstance of life,
If I could only be his wife.
His manly form and pleasant face,
His winsome ways and gentle grace,
And most of all his christian zeal,
Doth like celestial magic steal
Through every recess of my heart,
With richest blessings to impart.
Silvanus I almost adore—
But hark! Some one is at the door.''

She quickly smoothed her glossy hair,
And soon regained her graceful air,
Then gently walked across the floor,
And met her father at the door,
Who just had come from Pleasantvale,
And brought their semi-weekly mail.
The fam'ly gathered round to see,
And each one asked: Is it for me?
'' This letter is,'' he said, '' for Ruth,
Mailed at the little town of Booth,
And I suspect some youth up there,
Of winsome way and taking air,

51

And conversation smooth and bland,
Thinks he can win her heart and hand."
Ruth took the letter, and with speed,
Ran to her room and did it read
With sweetly tinted blushing face,
That stole the roses from their vase.
With throbbing heart she then began,
And read the letter o'er again,
And as she folded up the sheet,
She said : '' My joy is now complete.
How glad I feel ! Yet strange indeed !
My feelings and my thoughts exceed
The power of my tongue to tell,
The joy that doth my bosom swell.
Yes, he has touched the living key
Of interchanging harmony,
And I will answer him to-night,
And fill his soul with sweet delight.
'Praise God from whom all blessings flow,
Praise him all creatures here below.' ''

That night Silvanus, so depressed
That he could neither sleep nor rest,

Began to thus soliloquize,
With throbbing heart and wakeful eyes :

Silvanus :
" My mind, to-night, is much annoyed
With doubts that I cannot avoid ;
For love, while kept in dread suspense,
Most takes away a person's sense.
What if my love should be in vain,
And she should treat it with disdain,
Or if, perchance, some other youth,
Has won the loving heart of Ruth ?
Oh how these thoughts perplex my mind,
And how the eyes of hope they blind !
The gleams of moonlight gently fall,
In silver sheen upon the wall.
The gentle zephyr sweetly sings,
And with her fragrant laden wings,
Attempts to drive away the gloom,
Of dismal shadows from my room ;
But yet to me no comfort comes,
Because grave doubts do beat their drums,
Whose loud and long sonorous tones,

Sound like a dying culprit's groans.
Oh, gentle zephyr, 'tis in vain
For you to try to ease my pain,
Or to relieve me from the blues,
Unless from Ruth you bring good news.
Oh could I hear from her to-night,
And did our hearts in love unite,
My heart would beat a double quick,
And with increasing gladness tick
This long and gloomy night away,
And muster in the welcome day !
But news, so soon, I can't expect,
And so must wait a while perplext.
True love's a passion of the soul,
Which mortal man cannot control.
E'n Sampson with his mighty arm,
Could not resist her Siren charm.
She sits upon her golden throne,
And all around are trophies strewn
From both our earthly hemispheres,
Which she retains as souvenirs
Of presents which she has received,

And victories by her achieved.
She conquers, not by force of arms,
But by her strong and graceful charms.
All nations worship at her shrine,
And kings to her their thrones resign.
The rich, the poor, the wise and great,
As willing courtiers on her wait,
For she's a benefactress kind,
Which God hath given to mankind.
True love is nature's balance wheel,
The fountain of domestic weal,
The sure preventive of divorce,
The source of social intercourse,
Of peace, good will and harmony,
And friendly reciprocity.''

And thus he mused away the hours,
Until the radiating show'rs
Of morning's dawn had drowned the night.
And drenched the earth with floods of light;
But yet his troubles were not drowned
Until the next day rolled around,
And then the looked for letter came

Which set his heart with joy aflame.
With trembling hands and dizzy head,
He opened it and quickly read
A message that dispelled his gloom
And drove the shadows from his room.
Then all his doubts in great dismay
And wild disorder fled away.
His mental clouds, so dark and weird,
Before his vision disappeared,
And he, with wonder and surprise,
Looked round upon the earth and skies,
And then exclaimed; "The scene has
    changed,
Or else my senses are deranged !
The sky has changed its lurid hue,
And now brings out its native blue ;
The verdant landscape looks serene,
And so doth all the wondrous scene.
The fiends, which last night on me frowned,
Are in the Stygian river drowned.
'Praise God from whom all blessings flow,
Praise him all creatures here below.'"

The courtship suit was now begun ;
And like the blazing morning sun,
Rejoicing to begin his race
Through regions of celestial space,
And feeling sure that he will win,
And take the prize with pleasure in,
So young Silvanus with a zeal
That blazed and flamed with hopeful weal,
Pressed hard his suit at Hymen's court,
Where he was now in good report.

The suit went on in proper style,
And weeks and months in single file
Brought round to them in golden cup,
From which they both as one did sup,
The pleasures of their courtship life
Without a single drop of strife.
Together they were often found,
As time, its cycles rolled around,
And often talked of that glad day,
When in the coming month of May.
They were at Hymen's court to bow,
And seal their happy marriage vow.

Their future plans were also laid,
And all their future prospects weighed,
Which prophesied a future bright,
As far as went their human sight.
But yet, should disappointments come,
With sword and shield, and fife and drum,
And in a heartless manner slay
These prospects in an hour or day,
They both agreed that Love would stand,
And bid defiance to the band,
And o'er their lifeless bodies tread,
To other prospects yet ahead.

The Summer, with her glowing smile,
Departed slowly for a while,
With perfumed robes and fragrant mouth,
Far down into the sunny south ;
But ere she went she left behind,
Rich blessings of a varied kind.
Then Autumn, with his golden fruit,
And nicely fitting yellow suit,
Stepped out of his abiding place,
And took the earth in his embrace,

Filled all her barns with ripened grain,
And then, with hope, went home again,
That Winter, with his snow and ice,
Might come and raise the market price.
Old Winter came with cold profuse,
And long white beard and snowy shoes,
And polar garments round him drawn,
And with a mighty giant's brawn,
Spread forth his blessings o'er the land,
With open and with lavish hand,
Together with some want and grief
For charity to find relief;
And then, with praises and some blame,
Returned again from whence he came,
To let a Maid from warmer climes,
Come forth with her enchanting chimes,
To wake the cold and sleeping earth,
And call it to a nobler birth .
Then lovely Spring, with rosy crown,
And green and flowing velvet gown,
With wreathes of flowers wrapped ar und,
Stepped out upon the barren ground

From her ambrosial palace hall,
Where winter never comes at all,
And spread her mantle o'er the earth,
And poured her oil into its dearth,
Until it looked like paradise
Before the blight of sin and vice .
She seemed to take some special pains
With her already gorgeous trains,
In view of that glad wedding day,
Set for the flow'ry month of May:
For she delights to do her best,
In north or south, or east or west,
For all who set their marriage day,
In either April or in May.

The wedding day soon rolled around,
And there was heard the joyful sound
Of happy voices in the trees,
And happy voices in the breeze,
And fast approaching buggy wheels,
Almost upon the horses' heels,
And nimble footmen coming near,
With anxious ears attuned to hear,

The verdict of the suit at court,
Which Hymen was to soon report.
The happy couple now inside—
Silvanus and his coming bride—
Were ready for the welcome hour,
To hear the voice of legal pow'r,
Approve what nature had decreed,
And they, themselves, had long agreed.
The friends of both were soon within,
And soon the verdict did begin,
(Which all agreed was just and right,)
That this young couple should unite,
As husband true and faithful wife,
Throughout their earthly term of life.
The bride and groom with cheerful grace,
Sat down at the appointed place.
Beneath an arch of flowers gay,
And looked more happy than the day.
Congratulations were profuse,
And presents for their future use;
And all were happy as the spring,
And made the cozy farm house ring,

With instrumental music rare,
And vocal strains which rent the air.
The guardian angels too, were there,
Invisible to all as air,
And with ecstatic voices sang,
Which to the arch of heaven rang :
" Praise God from whom all blessings flow;
Praise Him all creatures here below;
Praise Him above, ye heavenly host;
Praise Father, Son and Holy Ghost."